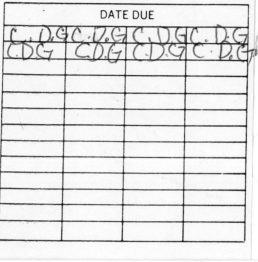

92
ELL
C¹ Bishop, Jack
Ralph Ellison

DATE DUE			

RALPH
ELLISON

RALPH ELLISON

·•◖◗•·

Jack Bishop

Senior Consulting Editor
Nathan Irvin Huggins
Director
W.E.B. Du Bois Institute for Afro-American Research
Harvard University

CHELSEA HOUSE PUBLISHERS
New York   Philadelphia

Editor-in-Chief Nancy Toff

Executive Editor Remmel T. Nunn

Managing Editor Karyn Gullen Browne

Copy Chief Juliann Barbato

Picture Editor Adrian G. Allen

Art Director Giannella Garrett

Manufacturing Manager Gerald Levine

Staff for RALPH ELLISON

Senior Editor Richard Rennert

Associate Editor Perry King

Editorial Assistant Laura-Ann Dolce

Copy Editor Gillian Bucky

Associate Picture Editor Juliette Dickstein

Picture Researcher Elie Porter

Senior Designer Laurie Jewell

Designer Teresa Clark

Cover Illustration Alan J. Nahigian

Creative Director Harold Steinberg

5   7   9   8   6   4

Library of Congress Cataloging in Publication Data
Bishop, Jack,
   Ralph Ellison.

   (Black Americans of achievement)
   Bibliography: p.
   Includes index.
   1. Ellison, Ralph—Biography—Juvenile literature.
2. Novelists, American—20th century—Biography—
Juvenile literature.   [1. Ellison, Ralph.   2. Authors,
American.   3. Afro-Americans—Biography]   I. Title.
II. Series.
PS3555.L625Z59   1988   818'.5409   [B]   [92]
87-15858

ISBN 1-55546-585-4
      0-7910-0202-0   (pbk.)

CONTENTS

BLACK
AMERICANS
OF
ACHIEVEMENT

Muhammad Ali
heavyweight champion

Richard Allen
*founder of the
African Methodist
Episcopal church*

Louis Armstrong
musician

James Baldwin
author

Benjamin Banneker
*scientist and
mathematician*

Mary McLeod Bethune
educator

Blanche K. Bruce
politician

Ralph Bunche
diplomat

George Washington Carver
botanist

Charles Waddell Chestnutt
author

Paul Cuffe
merchant and abolitionist

Frederick Douglass
abolitionist editor

Charles R. Drew
physician

W.E.B. Du Bois
scholar and activist

Paul Laurence Dunbar
poet

Duke Ellington
bandleader and composer

Ralph Ellison
author

Ella Fitzgerald
singer

Marcus Garvey
black-nationalist leader

Prince Hall
social reformer

William H. Hastie
educator and politician

Matthew A. Henson
explorer

Chester Himes
author

Billie Holiday
singer

John Hope
educator

Lena Horne
entertainer

Langston Hughes
poet

James Weldon Johnson
author

Scott Joplin
composer

Martin Luther King, Jr.
civil rights leader

Joe Louis
heavyweight champion

Malcolm X
militant black leader

Thurgood Marshall
Supreme Court justice

Elijah Muhammad
religious leader

Jesse Owens
champion athlete

Gordon Parks
photographer

Sidney Poitier
actor

Adam Clayton Powell, Jr.
political leader

A. Philip Randolph
labor leader

Paul Robeson
singer and actor

Jackie Robinson
baseball great

John Russwurm
publisher

Sojourner Truth
antislavery activist

Harriet Tubman
antislavery activist

Nat Turner
slave revolt leader

Denmark Vesey
slave revolt leader

Madame C. J. Walker
entrepreneur

Booker T. Washington
educator

Walter White
political activist

Richard Wright
author

ON ACHIEVEMENT

————— ❧ —————

Coretta Scott King

BEFORE YOU BEGIN this book, I hope you will ask yourself what the word excellence means to you. I think that it's a question we should all ask, and keep asking as we grow older and change. Because the truest answer to it should never change. When you think of excellence, perhaps you think of success at work; or of becoming wealthy; or meeting the right person, getting married, and having a good family life.

Those important goals are worth striving for, but there is a better way to look at excellence. As Martin Luther King, Jr., said in one of his last sermons, "I want you to be first in love. I want you to be first in moral excellence. I want you to be first in generosity. If you want to be important, wonderful. If you want to be great, wonderful. But recognize that he who is greatest among you shall be your servant."

My husband, Martin Luther King, Jr., knew that the true meaning of achievement is service. When I met him, in 1952, he was already ordained as a Baptist preacher and was working towards a doctoral degree at Boston University. I was studying at the New England Conservatory and dreamed of accomplishments in music. We married a year later, and after I graduated the following year we moved to Montgomery, Alabama. We didn't know it then, but our notions of achievement were about to undergo a dramatic change.

You may have read or heard about what happened next. What began with the boycott of a local bus line grew into a national movement, and by the time he was assassinated in 1968 my husband had fashioned a black movement powerful enough to shatter forever the practice of racial segregation. What you may not have read about is where he got his method for resisting injustice without compromising his religious beliefs.

He got the strategy of nonviolence from a man of a different race, who lived in a distant country, and even practiced a different religion. The man was Mahatma Gandhi, the great leader of India, who devoted his life to serving humanity in the spirit of love and nonviolence. It was in these principles that Martin discovered his method for social reform. More than anything else, those two principles were the key to his achievements.

This book is about black Americans who served society through the excellence of their achievements. It forms a part of the rich history of black men and women in America—a history of stunning accomplishments in every field of human endeavor, from literature and art to science, industry, education, diplomacy, athletics, jurisprudence, even polar exploration.

Not all of the people in this history had the same ideals, but I think you will find something that all of them have in common. Like Martin Luther King, Jr., they all decided to become "drum majors" and serve humanity. In that principle—whether it was expressed in books, inventions, or song—they found something outside themselves to use as a goal and a guide. Something that showed them a way to serve others, instead of living only for themselves.

Reading the stories of these courageous men and women not only helps us discover the principles that we will use to guide our own lives, but it teaches us about our black heritage and about America itself. It is crucial for us to know the heroes and heroines of our history and to realize that the price we paid in our struggle for equality in America was dear. But we must also understand that we have gotten as far as we have partly because America's democratic system and ideals made it possible.

We still are struggling with racism and prejudice. But the great men and women in this series are a tribute to the spirit of our democratic ideals and the system in which they have flourished. And that makes their stories special, and worth knowing. ☙

RALPH
ELLISON

1

GREAT EXPECTATIONS

❦

YOUNG AND FULL of hope, Ralph Ellison moved in 1936 from Alabama to the area in New York City known as Harlem. Regarded as the black capital of America almost since the turn of the century, Harlem then stood as a symbol of racial progress, attracting black immigrants from all over the world.

Before blacks began to live in Harlem in the early 1900s, it was a small village along the northern outskirts of New York City inhabited by a mixture of wealthy and working-class whites. It had tree-lined streets and mansions surrounded by handsome lawns, and it contained a large number of attractive townhouses and brownstones. Yet many of these apartments were empty. Real-estate developers had been so anxious to build housing in this desirable community that they had constructed more homes in Harlem than there were tenants to fill them.

In the early 1900s blacks began to move from the West Side of New York into these available Harlem apartments which were priced at agreeable rents. They were eager to escape from the racial violence and poor living conditions that were commonplace in the congested West Side ghettos where they had been living for decades.

As Harlem grew as a black community in the early 1900s, blacks established a wide variety of businesses catering to the growing population.

W. E. B. Du Bois helped to found the National Association for the Advancement of Colored People in 1909 and then edited its publication, Crisis, for 25 years.

Most blacks had come to New York expecting it to be some kind of paradise. The poet Paul Laurence Dunbar wrote in 1902, "All the days of their lives they had heard about it, and it seemed to them the center of all the glory, all the wealth, and all the freedom of the world." Yet upon their arrival in New York, they were refused housing in almost all parts of the city. Such refusals forced rich and poor blacks alike to live together in the only housing that was offered to them: the tenements on the city's West Side.

The overdevelopment of Harlem dramatically changed the living situation for most blacks in New York. From 1910 to 1920, the black population in Harlem grew to such an extent that the district soon became the most heavily populated black residential area in the United States. New York was not the only northern city to offer its black residents the opportunity to live in a growing, closely knit community; cities such as Cleveland, Ohio, and Chicago, Illinois, also attracted black migrants from the rural South who were looking for jobs in the industrial North. But with its excellent available housing, Harlem could offer its residents the promise of an unusually high quality of life; and as it became crowded with black institutions and organizations, Harlem also gave its residents the opportunity to be a part of the most exciting and cosmopolitan city in the United States. According to the clergyman Adam Clayton Powell, Sr., Harlem in the 1920s "became the symbol of liberty and the Promised Land to Negroes everywhere."

Among the many blacks who came to live in this growing community were such well-respected men of letters as W. E. B. Du Bois, James Weldon Johnson, and Claude McKay. They joined with other authors, actors, and musicians to turn Harlem into an intellectual and artistic center for blacks. This period of artistic achievement came to be known as the Harlem Renaissance. The writer Arna Bontemps said, "We were heralds of a dawning day. We were the first-born of the dark renaissance." By focusing their energies on black subjects, participants in the Harlem Renaissance were among the first American artists to praise black culture and promote black values.

The generally upbeat mood of most Harlemites during the time of the Harlem Renaissance came to an end when the stock market crash of 1929 was followed by the Great Depression. Nearly half of the 200,000 people who were living in Harlem in 1930 eventually required some form of unemployment relief. The effects of poverty were visible throughout

Adam Clayton Powell, Sr., was the most prominent clergyman in Harlem from the early 1900s until his retirement in 1937. His son Adam (in center) inherited the elder Powell's pulpit before embarking on a political career.

The most popular music center in Harlem for many years, the Lafayette Theatre was also the home of the district's first theater group, the Lafayette Players.

the black community, and what had once been one of New York's most beautiful areas began to deteriorate as tenants unable to pay their rents were forced out of their apartments and onto the streets.

Yet Harlem's reputation as a center of black arts and letters managed to remain intact throughout the 1930s. Through the efforts of artists such as Augusta Savage and writers such as Countee Cullen, Harlem continued to attract the prominent as well as the hopeful to its streets.

Twenty-two-year-old Ralph Ellison was among those who came to Harlem with great expectations. After he completed his third year of college at Tuskegee Institute in Alabama, there was a mix-up concerning his tuition fee for the following year. Convinced that he could not earn enough money to pay for the fee in economically depressed Alabama, he decided to go to New York for the summer, where he believed he could earn the necessary money.

Ellison was majoring in music and music theory in college, although his artistic interests also included literature, photography, and sculpture. He hoped that he would be able to focus on his true talent and begin to establish his career as an artist by spending a summer in New York. "I thought of it," he said, "as the freest of American cities and considered Harlem as the site and symbol of Afro-American progress and hope." Like many who had come to Harlem before him, this admittedly "eager, young, celebrity-fascinated college junior" looked to learn from the community's leading artistic figures.

Ellison arrived in Harlem on June 5, 1936, with $75 in his pockets and his head filled with dreams of becoming a successful artist. The next day, he encountered two of black America's leading figures, Alain Locke and Langston Hughes, on the steps of the Harlem YMCA.

The writer Arna Bontemps came to Harlem from Los Angeles in 1924 and soon became one of the central figures in the Harlem Renaissance.

A noted philosopher and educator, Locke was educated at Harvard University as well as at Oxford University in England, where he became America's first black Rhodes scholar. He then became a professor at Howard University in Washington, D.C. Among his many accomplishments, he was the editor of *The New Negro*, an important anthology of black fiction, poetry, drama, and essays that had been published in 1925.

In this groundbreaking work, which Ellison had read while he was in high school, Locke argued that a new breed of black Americans was emerging during the 1920s. *The New Negro* noted that the migration of blacks from the rural South to cities in the North brought together blacks of various backgrounds. Their

The poet Langston Hughes (shown here) played an instrumental role in Ellison's career: he was responsible for bringing together Ellison and author Richard Wright.

exchange of ideas and folklore was responsible for producing a "New Negro," urban and sophisticated. According to Locke, the New Negro was interested in the visual arts as well as music and literature, and in many ways resembled Ellison's ideal of what a man should be.

Ellison had been introduced to Locke at Tuskegee only a few weeks before spotting him on the steps of the YMCA. With the memory of this previous meeting fresh in his mind, Ellison walked up to Locke and asked him, "Dr. Locke, do you remember me?"

"Why, of course I do," Locke said. He then proceeded to introduce Ellison to Langston Hughes, one of Harlem's most celebrated poets, who incorporated elements of jazz and blues music into his poems, and wrote in vivid images about all aspects of daily black life.

Scholar and teacher Alain Locke, one of the most respected intellectuals in the black community, did his best to champion the efforts of the members of the Harlem Renaissance.

The conversation between Ellison, Locke, and Hughes quickly turned to the subject of literature— a topic that excited Ellison. While working in the library at Tuskegee, he had seen his boyhood love for books flourish. "I'd become fascinated by the exciting developments that were taking place in modern literature," he said.

One of these major developments was the use of a narrative style that did not tell a story in a conventional manner. At Locke's suggestion, Hughes offered to lend Ellison two novels that were written in this style. They were *Man's Fate* and *The Days of Wrath*, by the French writer André Malraux.

When Ellison later returned these books to Hughes, he asked the poet if he knew the writer Richard Wright personally. Ellison had read one of Wright's poems in a politically radical magazine called *New Masses* and had been so captivated by Wright's work that it became for him a literary model. "Indeed," Ellison said, "such reading and wondering prepared me not only to *meet* Wright, but to seek him out."

French writer André Malraux was one of the central figures in the modern literary movement that fascinated Ellison while he was in college.

Hughes not only told Ellison that he knew Wright, but secretly wrote to Wright to tell him about Ellison's admiration. Much to Ellison's surprise, he soon received a postcard from Wright himself. The message from Wright began: "Langston Hughes tells me that you're interested in meeting me. I will be in New York [in July]." Wright was in the process of moving from Chicago to New York to become the editor of *New Challenge* magazine as well as to join the Harlem bureau's staff of the *Daily Worker*, a Communist newspaper.

While Wright was preparing to come to New York, Ellison was discovering that the city was an intriguing place for a young man who had lived in the South and Southwest for his entire life. The subways especially interested him as places where blacks and whites, rich and poor mingled beneath the city's streets. Above ground, he did not have to ride in the back of the bus, as blacks were forced to do in the South.

Ellison's home during his first few months in New York was the Harlem YMCA, where many young artists lived. Rent at the YMCA was very low, and this low cost was very welcome because jobs were scarce in New York due to the depression. Ellison worked as a counterman at the YMCA's restaurant, and he later took a job as a receptionist and file clerk for an eminent psychiatrist, Harry Stack Sullivan. Although Ellison only worked briefly for Sullivan, he

The depression in the 1930s left its mark on all of New York—not just Harlem. Programs such as the one shown below were instituted to provide food and relief.

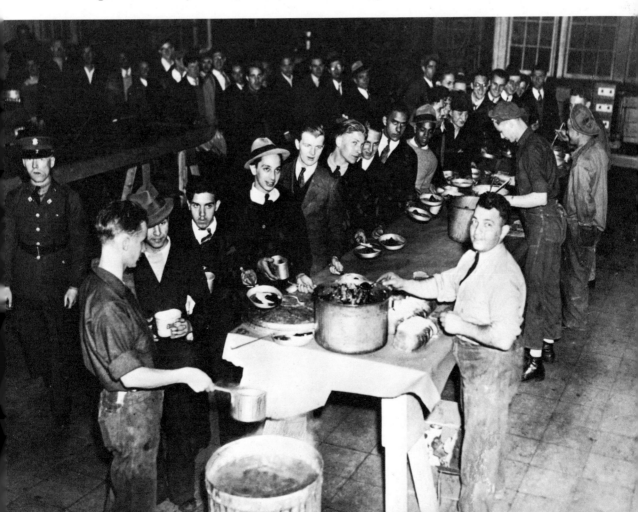

Psychiatrist Harry Stack Sullivan provided Ellison with one of the most interesting jobs that he held during the depression.

said that this job was "one of the most interesting I ever had." While working for the doctor, he was able to glance through the records of Sullivan's famous patients. Ellison's experiences in the doctor's office also prompted him to reread the works of Sigmund Freud and other influential psychoanalysts of the day.

Like most of the jobs that Ellison was able to find during the summer of 1936, this one paid very little and lasted for only a short time. He eventually worked at several factories, but these jobs also were low paying, and he was soon forced to spend many nights sleeping on park benches. Flat broke, he was unable to return to Tuskegee that fall.

After journeying home in the late winter to attend his mother's funeral, Ellison returned to New York in the spring of 1937 and found the job market to be no different than it had been before he left the city. However, being unemployed gave him the chance to spend time with Wright. Ellison said of Wright, "He had as much curiosity about how writing is written as I had about how music is composed, and our curiosity concerning artistic creation became the basis of our friendship." Ellison often visited Wright in his office at the *Daily Worker*, where he talked to him about books, music, and politics, and also had an opportunity to read many of Wright's unpublished works. These stories would later gain much attention for their author, as would Wright's longer works *Uncle Tom's Children*, *Native Son*, and *Black Boy*.

Wright eventually asked Ellison to write a book review on Waters Edward Turpin's novel *These Low Grounds* for the first issue of *New Challenge*. Ellison later said, "To one who had never attempted to write anything, this was the wildest of ideas." Printed in the fall of 1937, the review became his first published work.

Wright then asked Ellison if he would write a short story. Ellison "went about writing rashly unaware that my ambitions as a composer had been fatally diverted." The result of this effort was "Hymie's Bull," a short story that Wright sought to get published.

The process of writing, Ellison discovered, helped him to address such questions as "Who am I, what am I, how did I come to be? What shall I make of the life around me, what celebrate, what reject?" In looking to answer these basic questions, he embarked on a lengthy literary career in which he examined his life and times. Among the results of this investigation is his novel, *Invisible Man*, a work so powerful and so popular that it has placed Ellison at the forefront of American writers in the 20th century. ❦

2

OKLAHOMA TERRITORY

R ALPH WALDO ELLISON was born on March 1, 1914, in Oklahoma City, Oklahoma. The second son of Lewis and Ida Ellison, he had an older brother who died while still an infant. Three years after Ralph was born, his parents had another son, Herbert.

An avid reader, Lewis Ellison chose to name his son after the 19th-century philosopher and writer Ralph Waldo Emerson as an act of faith in his son's future. He believed that Ralph was going to be a poet. But Ralph never really felt comfortable with being named after this great American. He thought the name carried too much history with it.

Emerson embodied in his writings a distinctly American philosophy which contends that each individual is responsible for his or her own destiny. When Ralph was a schoolboy, he read Emerson's "Concord Hymn" and his essay on "Self-Reliance," and felt that the pressure to become a great man like Emerson was so strong that he decided never to read any of his writings again. Ralph also shortened his middle name to the initial "W." Yet his full given name has actually proven to be very fitting for a man whose life has shown that hard work and dedication to individual principles can lead to success.

Oklahoma in the 1890s and early 1900s was a land of promise to black settlers hoping to start life anew in an environment relatively free of racial discrimination.

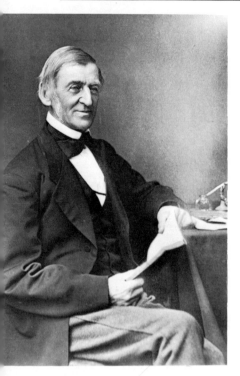

Ralph Waldo Emerson is celebrated for having developed a truly American philosophy of self-reliance.

Ralph's parents came to Oklahoma from the Deep South. His mother was born on a farm in White Oak, Georgia, and his father was born in Abbeville, South Carolina. As a young man, Lewis Ellison enlisted in the army, eventually fighting in Cuba, China, and the Philippines. After returning to Abbeville, he worked in an ice cream parlor. He met Ida Milsap in Abbeville while she was visiting some relatives. Soon after their marriage, they moved to Chattanooga, Tennessee, in 1909. There Lewis ran a candy kitchen with his brother, worked in a restaurant, and was employed by a construction firm. However, like so many other Americans at the time, Lewis and Ida Ellison soon decided to move farther west, to Oklahoma, where there were more opportunities for a better life. Although slavery was abolished by President Abraham Lincoln in 1863, racial injustice continued to trouble blacks throughout the United States.

The area now known as Oklahoma had once been the home of several Indian tribes that had been forced westward during the 1830s by the federal government. When the Oklahoma Territory was opened for general settlement in 1889, impoverished blacks were offered the chance at a new life in a new state without a history of slavery or segregation. At the end of Mark Twain's novel *The Adventures of Huckleberry Finn*, which was first published in 1884, Huck Finn says, "I got to light out for the Territory." Twain's famous novel about the clash of white and black cultures in the South ends with Huck deciding to move west to Oklahoma, in an attempt to escape the slave society of the South.

During the 1890s and early 1900s, thousands of settlers, both black and white, moved to Oklahoma, where great expanses of undeveloped land made the state seem like it was on the edge of the American frontier. White settlers soon brought their prejudices with them, and discriminatory laws were subsequently

The Emancipation Proclamation issued on September 22, 1862, was one of the steps that President Abraham Lincoln took to abolish racial injustice in the United States.

Oklahoma City, Oklahoma, on April 22, 1889—two hours before it was opened for settlement. The population of Oklahoma City went from zero to 10,000 by the end of the day.

enacted. These new laws restricted the movement of black citizens by denying them access to certain restaurants, theaters, and stores. Under these laws, known as Jim Crow laws, everything from bathrooms to water fountains could be designated for use by whites only.

Despite the Jim Crow laws, Oklahoma offered more opportunities to blacks than were generally available in the Deep South. Lewis Ellison found work in Oklahoma, first as a construction foreman, then by selling ice and coal. As the years passed, it seemed as though his growing family would have a bright future in Oklahoma. However, Lewis Ellison never lived to see this happen. He was killed in an accident in 1917, leaving his wife to raise their two young sons.

Ida Ellison began working as a maid in several homes in Oklahoma City to support her two sons. Although she had only finished the eighth grade, she was determined to provide them with an education. She was also an ardent supporter of Eugene Debs's Socialist party and became involved in local politics, much as her son Ralph would after moving to New York. She eventually became the superintendent of several apartment houses in Oklahoma City, and in 1934 she was jailed briefly for attempting to rent apartments to blacks, which under Jim Crow laws were reserved for whites.

Throughout Ralph's childhood, his mother was too poor to buy him many presents. Instead, she brought home dozens of discarded records, books, and magazines from the homes where she worked. Ralph spent hours looking through these materials, reading about faraway places and people. He said, "They spoke to me of a life which was broader and more interesting, and although it was not really a part of my own life, I never thought they were not for me simply because I happened to be Negro. They were things which spoke of a world which I could some day make my own."

This advertisement for the Social Democratic party of America features the party's founder, Eugene Debs, who ran for the presidency of the United States five times between 1900 and 1920.

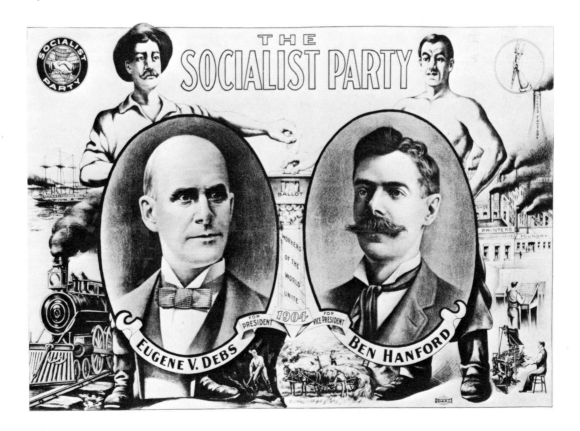

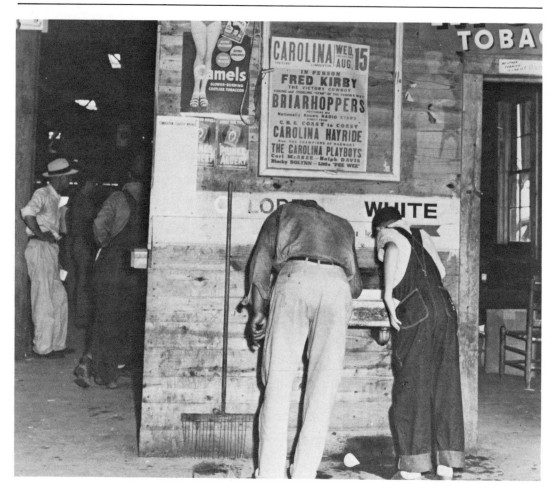

The passage of Jim Crow laws sanctioned racial segregation in all aspects of life in the United States.

These books, magazines, and records succeeded in exposing Ralph to the world beyond Oklahoma City, which to Ellison "appeared to be in the same class with say Kansas City or St. Louis or Chicago—only it was much smaller and very much better." By presenting him with these gifts, his mother did not dwell on the racial and economic barriers that Ralph would most probably face in life; rather, she continually reinforced the notion that success was possible if he worked to make his dreams come true.

These notions of achievement eventually prompted Ralph to strive toward an ideal known as the "Renaissance man," a well-rounded individual with

knowledge of various artistic and scientific disciplines. The concept of the Renaissance man dates
back to 15th-century Italy—the period known as the
Renaissance—when there was a revival of classical
learning and renewed interest in the civilizations of
ancient Greece and Rome. Many Europeans subsequently began to model themselves on the classical
ideal of the multitalented individual.

Ralph later said:

As a kid I remember working it out this way: there was
a world in which you wore your everyday clothes on
Sunday, and there was a world in which you wore your
Sunday clothes every day—I wanted the world in which
you wore your Sunday clothes every day. I wanted it
because it represented something better, a more exciting and civilized and human way of living, a world
which came to me through certain scenes of felicity
which I encountered in fiction, in the movies, and
which I glimpsed sometimes through the windows of
great houses on Sunday afternoons when my mother
took my brother and me for walks through the wealthy
white sections of the city. I know it now for a boy's
vague dream of possibility.

*Viewing the residences of the rich
in Oklahoma City made Ellison
dream, he said, of "a world
which I glimpsed sometimes
through the windows of great
houses on Sunday afternoons."*

Ellison's hometown, Oklahoma City, proved to be a fascinating place in which to grow up in the early 1900s.

He also believed that by living a life of accomplishment he could escape from the world of poverty.

More than simply influencing Ralph's notions of success and accomplishment, the ideal of the Renaissance man played a major role in shaping his perceptions of race relations. As a boy growing up without a father, he was constantly in search of father figures and role models. When he tried to imagine what the ideal Renaissance man was like, he pictured someone who was "neither white nor black, Christian nor Jewish, but representative of certain desireable essences, of skills and powers physical, aesthetic and moral." He came to believe that success could be measured by certain standards of achievement that had nothing to do with race. His willingness to recognize and judge people, black or white, by their abilities and not their race or religion became a large factor in establishing himself as a success.

When Ralph was a boy, he liked to fish and hunt with his brother. He also liked to play with mechanical objects, especially radios. His mother often brought home radio magazines from the homes where she worked as a maid, and he would try to build the radios he saw in these magazines from spare parts he found in garbage cans. He often would spend hours looking through his neighbors' garbage for old appliances. He would bring them home, take them apart, and then use some of the odd parts to build his radios.

One day while Ralph was looking for spare parts, he met a white boy named Hoolie next to a trash container. Hoolie, who was also interested in radios, was looking for spare parts too. Ralph offered him some of his findings, and the two boys quickly became friends. They began to spend a lot of time together, talking about radios and shortwave communications. Because Hoolie had a severe heart condition, he was unable to attend school and had to stay at home most afternoons. Having few playmates, he was especially happy to have met Ralph. For Ralph, it was important to meet another boy whose intellectual interests matched his own.

Although Ralph and Hoolie came from very different backgrounds, they were united by their interest in radios. The fact that Hoolie came from a relatively wealthy white family and was the son of a prominent Episcopal pastor proved to Ralph that ability—not race—could bring people together. He learned to be accepting of other people throughout his life, searching for a commitment to excellence in others regardless of their race. ◆

3
THE SOUND OF MUSIC

WHILE still a youth, Ralph helped his family make ends meet by taking a series of after-school jobs. He worked as a delivery boy for a pharmacy, as a sales clerk for a haberdasher, and as a newspaper delivery boy. Besides providing Ralph with a little spending money, these jobs introduced him to many members of Oklahoma City's black community.

Among the most influential of these people was J. D. Randolph, a janitor at the Oklahoma State Law Library. Ralph worked as Randolph's assistant and learned many things from this man of many accomplishments. Earlier in his life, Randolph had walked all the way from Tennessee to Oklahoma, where he helped to found one of the state's first schools. He knew many fascinating details about Oklahoma's legal code and often told Ralph stories about specific cases and their legal significance. Although Randolph never complained about his job to Ralph, the 11-year-old soon came to realize that such a learned man should not have had to work as a janitor simply because he was black.

Randolph's two sons ran a drugstore on the corner of Stiles Avenue and Second Street in Oklahoma City's black neighborhood. Situated at the bottom of a long hill, the area around the store was called Deep

When Ellison was a teenager, he attended Douglass High School, which was named after the well-known abolitionist Frederick Douglass.

33

Second. The area was the central commercial district in Oklahoma City's black community, and the drugstore served as a gathering place for local residents. Ralph worked for a time at this store, which was just around the corner from his home.

The city's black musicians congregated at the drugstore to talk about jazz as well as to play it. Between making ice cream sodas and delivering prescriptions, Ralph often listened to the music of his favorite band, the Blue Devils Orchestra (which eventually became part of Count Basie's band). When Ralph later tried to make a career for himself as a musician, many of his friends from these days at the drugstore would help their longtime fan find work.

At the age of 16, Ralph began to attend Douglass High School, named after the slave-turned-abolitionist Frederick Douglass. The principal of the school

Ellison often listened to jazz music while he worked at a drugstore after school. His favorite jazz band was the Blue Devils Orchestra, which later became part of Count Basie's band (shown here).

was Inman Page, a well-known educator who had once been a slave. He graduated as class orator from Brown University in 1877. Ralph said of Page, "He was so dominant a figure during my school days that his voice and image are still evoked by certain passages of the Bible."

When Ralph was in high school he frequently joined the rest of the student body in the school's auditorium for chapel services. One day he and some other students were seated on a platform on the auditorium stage, behind Page, who was conducting a religious service. The boys were free to engage in horseplay because Page had his back to them. Ralph started to fool around with another student, and suddenly he was collared by Page. Ralph instinctively grabbed the nearby ropes that controlled the stage curtain. The two figures instantly went swinging around

According to Ellison, his longtime music instructor Zelia Breaux "introduced me to the basic discipline required of an artist."

the stage—until Ralph lost his grip on the rope and they tumbled to the floor, with Page landing on top of Ralph.

"What do you think you're doing, boy," Page yelled. "What do you think you're doing?"

He gave a mysterious little laugh as he helped Ralph to his feet, and then he chased Ralph out of the auditorium.

"And don't come back! Don't you dare come back!" he yelled.

Ralph later said, "It was a rough moment for me, a fall into chaos and disgrace, with the student body roaring its delight." Yet he was readmitted to the school on the following day—Page's little laugh had been a signal that he too had been fooling around, just like the boys.

But Ralph had learned his lesson. "I returned and managed to keep out of serious trouble from that day until I graduated," he said. "That one chaotic contact with authority was enough for me."

Page's daughter, Zelia N. Breaux, was the supervisor of music instruction for Oklahoma City's black schools. Ralph began his musical studies with her when he was in the second grade, and she was to remain his teacher and friend for many years. Under her direction, Ralph studied classical music and learned to play several brass instruments, including the trumpet and the saxophone. He devoted most of his study time to the trumpet and eventually became the first-chair trumpet in school as well as the band's student conductor.

Ralph supplemented his school education by taking private music lessons from Ludwig Hebestreit, the conductor of the Oklahoma City Orchestra. In exchange for cutting Hebestreit's lawn, Ralph received trumpet lessons as well as instruction in the technical aspects of symphonic composition. He also had discussions with Hebestreit about his work at the city orchestra and about the lives and music of Hebes-treit's favorite composers, Ludwig Van Beethoven, Richard Wagner, and Robert Schumann. It was during this time that Ralph set his first major goal: to write a symphony by the time he was 26 years old.

In addition to developing a strong background in classical music, Ralph was also a student of jazz, the blues, and gospel music. The Ellisons lived near a jazz hall, and Ralph often lay in bed at night, listening to the Blue Devils Orchestra and other local bands as the sound of their music wafted through his window. Ralph's mother was an active member of the Afro-American Methodist Episcopalian church, and it was there that he learned traditional Negro spirituals and hymns.

While Ellison attended Douglass High School, he participated in musical assemblies much like this one directed by Zelia Breaux.

When bandleader Duke Ellington (shown holding a baton) and his orchestra visited Oklahoma City, they immediately impressed Ellison. "They were news from the great wide world," he wrote, "an example and a goal."

When Ralph was a teenager, he played in several jazz bands, and he often went to performances at the Aldridge Theater and at Slaughter's Hall, where he came into contact with the music of black popular culture. Among the many performances he attended, perhaps Duke Ellington's visit to Oklahoma City was the most important for him. Ellington and his band arrived in town exhibiting their fancy clothes and sophisticated ways. They were concrete examples of the successful men Ralph had read about in books and magazines.

Ralph had come to know Ellington's music from the many records his mother brought home. He felt that Ellington "had taken the traditional instruments of Negro American music and modified them, extended their range, and enriched the tonal possibilities." Ellington's new mix of music included the use of muted brass instruments along with such ordinary household objects as toilet plungers. He showed, Ralph later said, that "jazz possessed the possibilities of range and expression comparable to that of classical music."

Thus, while Zelia Breaux taught Ralph the fundamentals of classical music and composition in school, Oklahoma City's black community educated him in the traditions of black music. Ralph later said that Breaux "introduced me to the basic discipline required of an artist," and this discipline and desire to become the best would help him to emerge as one of America's most important novelists of the 20th century. But it was the jazz sensibilities that he was exposed to in the shops of Deep Second that forever colored his notions of style and expression. ◖◗

Musician Louis Armstrong was much admired by Ellison. He wrote of the great trumpeter in Invisible Man, "I like Louis Armstrong because he's unaware that he is invisible."

4

HEADING
SOUTH

❦

WHILE ELLISON was in high school, he dedicated much time to athletics and schoolwork along with his music. He was a member of the football team, where he played both tackle and running back, and he was a consistently good student. However, by the time of his graduation from high school at the age of 19, it was not his athletic or scholastic achievements but his musical abilities that won him an Oklahoma State Scholarship to attend the prestigious black college in Alabama known as the Tuskegee Institute.

Before Ellison went to Tuskegee, he needed to buy some new clothes and a trumpet (the one he had used in high school belonged to the school). He worked for a while as an elevator operator to pay for these items, but paying for them cost him all of his meager savings. Unable to afford the train fare to Alabama, he decided to travel illegally. With the company of a family friend named Charlie, he set out for Alabama in June 1933.

Ellison and Charlie rode on freight trains all the way to St. Louis, Missouri. Charlie taught Ellison how to sneak aboard trains and how to jump off them. By the time they got to St. Louis, Ellison had mastered the trick of jumping on and off a moving train.

Like his fellow students who attended Tuskegee Institute in Alabama, Ellison found that the all-black university offered a wide range of courses.

Ellison was wary of traveling through the South in 1933, when racial tensions were great, due in large part to the trial of the Scottsboro Boys (shown here in jail).

In St. Louis, he said goodbye to Charlie—and to his past—and he continued alone on his journey.

While passing through Decatur, Alabama, Ellison was taken off a train with a group of other so-called hobos by two white railroad detectives. He was very scared because he knew that the Scottsboro Boys trial was taking place in Decatur. In that controversial case, a group of black boys had been accused of raping two white girls on a freight train. The case aroused anti-black feelings and random violence throughout the South. Ellison had read newspaper accounts of the trial and, like many people, was convinced that the defendants were not receiving a fair trial. He had also read about innocent blacks who were killed or beaten by whites retaliating in the name of the two alleged rape victims.

Fearing that he would become the victim of such violence, Ellison climbed off the train and joined the 40 or 50 other hobos. The two detectives, each armed

with a nickel-plated .45 revolver, forced the whites
and blacks to line up in the Decatur rail yard. When
Ellison saw a group of white boys suddenly attempt
to escape, he quickly followed them. He then hid
under a shed for several hours until he thought it was
safe to continue on. For a boy used to relative harmony between races in Oklahoma, this was an early
indication that life in the Deep South was going to
be different.

Fortunately for Ellison, he was "disciplined to
endure the absurdities of both conscious and unconscious prejudice, to resist racial provocation and, before the ready violence of brutal policemen, railroad
'bulls,' and casual white citizens, to hold my peace
and bide my time." But his stalwartness had a price.
As a frontier boy with a certain amount of city know-
how, he always felt as though he were a stranger in
Alabama, where life was filled with tradition and rural

*While Ellison attended Tuskegee
Institute, he occasionally left the
campus to perform in various jazz
clubs in the South.*

ways. Almost five percent of Tuskegee's students were from Oklahoma, yet Ellison never managed to feel comfortable with the mostly southern student body. In Oklahoma City there had been some interaction between blacks and whites. In Alabama, contact between the races was limited.

For the most part, Tuskegee students stayed on campus. When they did venture into town, their movements were heavily restricted. For example, the local movie theater was actually two theaters: one for white customers and the other for blacks. The two auditoriums were divided by a thin wall, and audiences watched the same films, but white and black patrons never saw each other—even in the lobby—because the films were shown at different times. Even though Oklahoma City also had adjacent yet separate movie houses for blacks and whites, the films were shown at the same time and both black and white patrons waited together in the lobby.

Ellison found it difficult to accept racial segregation in the South, where blacks and whites were not even allowed to mix in the lobby of a movie theater.

Ellison's experiences during his three years at Tuskegee would later form the basis of the first half of his novel *Invisible Man* . He said of this period in his life:

> I learned to outmaneuver those who interpreted my silence as submission, my efforts at self-control as fear, my contempt as awe before superior status, my dreams of faraway places and room at the top of the heap as a defeat before the barriers of their stifling provincial world. And my struggle became a desperate battle which was usually fought, though not always, in silence; a guerrilla action in a larger war in which I found some of the most treacherous assaults against me committed by those who regarded themselves either as neutrals, as sympathizers, or as disinterested military advisers.

Ellison considered himself an outsider throughout his time at Tuskegee, and found his college years to be a struggle to define himself—not only as an artist, but also in relation to both black and white cultures. He felt alienated from both the white society that surrounded Tuskegee and the black culture that had produced the school he so cherished. This sense of isolation led him to introspection and self-reliance, two traits he would carry with him when he left the South in 1936. He said, "In time I was to leave the South although it has never left me, and the interests which I discovered there became my life."

To understand the pressure Ellison felt at Tuskegee, it is necessary to know something about the college's history. Founded in 1881 by Booker T. Washington, Tuskegee soon became known as one of the South's premier universities for blacks. It was in a Tuskegee laboratory that George Washington Carver conducted his famous agricultural research. Tuskegee was modeled after Booker T. Washington's beloved alma mater, the Hampton Institute in Virginia. Like Hampton, Tuskegee was originally a trade school designed to educate young men and women for careers as teachers, church leaders, and domestics.

A leading spokesman for blacks at the turn of the century, educator Booker T. Washington founded prestigious Tuskegee Institute in a run-down church building.

Scientist George Washington Carver was asked by Booker T. Washington in 1896 to come to Tuskegee Institute, where the agricultural expert proceeded to conduct some of his most important research.

During the early years of the school, the emphasis was on vocational and technical skills rather than on academics. Washington believed that as tradespeople, blacks could provide whites with vital services and thereby provide a basis for racial harmony. Washington was popular with many southern whites largely because of his willingness to observe the traditions of segregation. An extremely optimistic man, he chose to ignore the many violent conflicts between the races and instead stressed the progress in society that black education had brought about since the Civil War.

When Washington founded Tuskegee, the school had very limited financial resources and the campus consisted of two poorly equipped buildings. However, by the time of his death in 1915, the campus featured 100 well-equipped buildings, which housed 1,500 students and 200 professors, and a healthy endowment of almost 2 million dollars. Washington was succeeded as Tuskegee's president in 1915 by his hand-picked successor, Robert Russa Moton. Tuskegee already had literature and music departments, but under Moton these and other liberal disciplines were strengthened.

In 1931 the Tuskegee School of Music was founded under the direction of William L. Dawson, a respected composer and classical musician. Ellison has referred to Dawson as "the greatest classical musician in that part of the country." The school of music was founded in order to provide black communities with music teachers, choir leaders, and concert performers. The school featured a choir of over 100 members, two glee clubs, and an orchestra.

When Ellison arrived at Tuskegee in June 1933, he saw no disadvantages in attending an all-black institution. The Tuskegee Choir was so well respected that it had performed at the opening of Radio City Music Hall in New York, an event which Ellison had read about in the papers while he was still in high school. Tuskegee's faculty was extremely well educated, and the facilities—including the library—were among the best in the South.

At Tuskegee Ellison worked toward fulfilling his childhood dream of composing a symphony. He majored in music and music theory, and he served for a time as student director of the school's orchestra, which traveled across the nation performing concerts. Like the music training given at Douglass High School, Tuskegee's music department offered an array of courses dealing with European musical tradition. Yet little formal instruction was available concerning the history of Afro-American music.

Booker T. Washington wanted Tuskegee students to be trained as domestics and tradespeople, believing that by performing necessary services for whites, blacks would be providing a foundation for racial harmony.

Along with some other students, Ellison satisfied his interest in Afro-American music by playing in several jazz bands. He often left Tuskegee to perform at clubs in Columbus, Georgia. Thus, his musical experiences at Tuskegee were in many ways a repetition of his experiences in Oklahoma City: in the classroom he received formal instruction in classical music, while out of school he learned about jazz.

In addition to his musical studies, Ellison took required courses in physical education and English. The head of Tuskegee's English department was Morteza Sprague, to whom Ellison later dedicated his second book, *Shadow and Act*, in 1964. Sprague taught a very popular course on the English novel which Ellison took during his sophomore year. However, it was by chance that he discovered what were to become for him the most important books he would ever read.

T. S. Eliot published his groundbreaking poem The Waste Land *in 1922. This work helped Ellison to see a common bond between literature and music.*

In order to make some extra spending money, Ellison took a part-time job in the college library, where he came across a series of books not taught by Tuskegee's English department. The works of American and European authors, these books were all part of the modernist movement in literature. The poetry of T. S. Eliot and Ezra Pound, the novels of Gertrude Stein and Ernest Hemingway, and the influential texts of Karl Marx (the founder of Marxism) and Sigmund Freud (the father of modern psychoanalysis) all helped open Ellison's eyes to the world beyond the segregated South. He said, "Books which seldom, if ever, mentioned Negroes were to release me from what ever 'segregated' idea I might have had of human possibilities." By reading about faraway places and people, he was encouraged once again to think beyond the limits imposed by his current situation.

Perhaps the single most important work that Ellison read at Tuskegee was T. S. Eliot's long poem, *The Waste Land*. Ellison came across this poem during his sophomore year, when he was 20 years old. He later said that the poem first revealed to him a connection between literature and jazz. *The Waste Land* helped him to see that the things that interested him about contemporary music could also be conveyed in literature. He said:

> "*The Waste Land* seized my mind. I was intrigued by its power to move me while eluding my understanding. Somehow its rhythms were often closer to those of jazz than were those of the Negro poets, and even though I could not understand then, its range of allusion was as mixed as varied as that of Louis Armstrong . . . and thus began my conscious education in literature.

After reading *The Waste Land*, Ellison began to read the work of one of America's best-known novelists of the period, Ernest Hemingway, and of Ireland's James Joyce. He soon began to write poetry,

Ellison said of Ernest Hemingway, "I find that he affirms the old American values by the eloquence of his denial; makes his moral point by stating explicitly that he does not believe in morality."

The technically rich works of the Irish writer James Joyce (shown here) encouraged Ellison to develop his own literary style.

and it was during this time that he first conceived of the idea of becoming a writer.

Although music was still Ellison's main interest during his years at Tuskegee, he also explored the visual arts as part of his Renaissance man ideal. He acted on stage, learned to paint, and began what would turn into a lifelong hobby of photography. He also began to take sculpture classes with Eva Hamlin, an art professor at Tuskegee. She introduced Ellison to clay sculpture and eventually helped encourage him to go to New York in the summer of 1936 to continue his sculpture studies.

By the time Ellison left Alabama to go to New York, he was sure that his future would be as an artist. Before he left Tuskegee, however, he learned an important lesson about what it takes to be a successful artist from Hazel Harrison, a teacher in the music department.

Harrison was one of Ellison's closest friends at Tuskegee. She was extremely talented and had studied in Berlin, Germany, with an important modern composer, Ferrucio Busoni. When Ellison was faced with adversity, he often turned to Harrison for understanding and advice.

One day after a particularly harsh critique of his monthly piano recital before various members of the music department, Ellison went to Harrison's studio seeking comfort. Still dressed in a rented tuxedo, which was the required attire for the recitals, Ellison listened as his friend and teacher told him a parable that would forever affect his work habits. The parable stressed how important it is for a person to try his best—even when he thinks no one is paying attention to him.

Ellison had been looking for sympathy when he approached Harrison, but instead he received a little lecture about accepting complete responsibility for not trying to play the piano hard enough during his recital.

"You must *always* play your best," she told him, "even if it's only in the waiting room at Chehaw Station, because in this country there'll always be a little man hidden behind the stove."

"A *what?*" Ellison asked.

"There'll always be a little man whom you don't expect, and he'll know the *music,* and the *tradition,* and the standards of *musicianship* required for whatever you set out to perform!" Her explanation left Ellison speechless.

He later said:

> After the working-over I'd just received from the faculty, I was in no mood for joking. But no, Miss Harrison's face was quite serious. So what did she mean? Chehaw Station was a lonely whistle-stop where swift north- or southbound trains paused with haughty impatience to drop off or take passengers; the point where, on homecoming weekends, special coaches crowded with festive visitors were cut loose, coupled to a waiting switch engine, and hauled to Tuskegee's railroad siding. I knew it well, and as I stood beside Miss Harrison's piano, visualizing the station, I told myself, *She has GOT to be kidding!*

However, the moral of Miss Harrison's lecture—that Ellison always try to do his best—fixed itself in his memory. It contained good advice that would prove useful in the days that lay ahead, when he would be leaving Tuskegee to join the crowds of people in New York. «»

While Ellison worked in the college library, he discovered the works of the leading figures in the modernist literary movement, including Ezra Pound (shown here).

5

THE
APPRENTICE

❧

ELLISON ARRIVED in New York in the spring of 1936. "New York," he said, "was one of the great cities prominent in the Negro American myth of freedom, a myth which goes back very far into Negro American experience. In our spirituals it was the North Star and places in the North which symbolized Freedom and to that extent I expected certain things from New York."

However, Ellison's first few months in Harlem were filled with difficulty and struggle; he found few jobs and earned little money. Despite such setbacks, the 22-year-old remained confident about his ability to become an artist. He took sculpture classes with two Harlem artists, Augusta Savage and Richmond Barthé, and worked at composing a symphony, while studying composition with Wallingford Riegger. He was still working toward the goal of writing a symphony by the time he was 26 years old.

Later in 1936, Ellison seemed to get the break that could launch his musical career. A friend of his who knew Duke Ellington offered to bring Ellison to Ellington's New York apartment. Ellison had been introduced to Ellington at Tuskegee, and he was anxious to become reacquainted with his childhood idol.

As luck would have it, Ellington invited Ellison to sit in on his band's rehearsal the following day. Ellison was thrilled by the possibility of playing with

"Harlem is a place where our folklore is preserved, and transformed," Ellison said of the district that he adopted as his home in 1936.

53

the most famous jazz band in the country, but his elation soon turned to disappointment when Ellington canceled the rehearsal. Hesitant to ask Ellington to renew his generous offer, Ellison turned to writing after his career as a musician failed to take off.

In February 1937, tragedy forced Ellison to leave New York. His mother, who had moved to Dayton, Ohio, had taken a bad fall and injured her hip. Later complications were misdiagnosed and she soon died.

After the funeral, Ellison and his brother, Herbert, stayed in Dayton for the rest of the winter. Both of them were broke, and they were forced to hunt quails to pay for their food. Using Hemingway's detailed stories about wing-shooting as their handbook, the two brothers became expert hunters. They sold most of their catch in order to buy basic foodstuff. They hunted during the day, and Ralph read and wrote at night. It was during these lean days and nights in Dayton that he resolved to become a writer.

It proved to be a cold and snowy winter. On one particularly snowy day, while the two brothers were hunting in a field owned by a friend's father, a red-faced farmer carrying a rifle suddenly emerged from behind a clump of trees. The sight of a white man running at them with a gun immediately frightened the two brothers, who began to prepare to defend themselves. They thought that their lives were in danger; as the farmer approached them, he looked as if he were planning to use his gun.

Herbert called out and told the farmer to stop. Realizing that the two hunters had misunderstood his intentions, the farmer quickly explained that he only wanted to warn them that they were trespassing on his neighbor's property. Herbert told him that they had permission to be there, and the farmer went away, satisfied. Yet his actions had almost provoked the two brothers to violence. The threat of violence would later serve Ellison as material in his fiction.

Sculptress Augusta Savage became well known during the Harlem Renaissance for serving as a mentor to a number of young artists—including Ellison.

Among Duke Ellington's admirers was Ellison, who "spent many a homesick afternoon playing Duke's records on the juke-box . . . asking myself why I was in New York and finding reassurance in the music."

During the spring of 1937, Ellison returned to New York. In June he befriended Richard Wright, who encouraged his efforts to become a writer. "And since Wright had assured me that I possessed a certain talent," Ellison said, "I decided that writing was the direction I would take."

In 1938 Ellison sought to land a job with the Federal Writers' Project. A government program sponsored by the Works Progress Administration (WPA), the Federal Writers' Project gave work to hundreds of writers throughout the country. The WPA had been set up by the government in 1935 to provide artists and artisans with useful employment. Schools and post offices were built, and paintings and sculptures were commissioned.

Few magazines and journals in 1938 published works written by blacks, so there were not many black professional writers at the time that the Federal Writers' Project was established. This was one of the reasons why few blacks were hired by the project. Racial discrimination by some of the project directors was another reason. However, men such as Sterling Brown, Editor of Negro Affairs for the project, and the diplomat Ralph Bunche campaigned for more blacks to be hired. And with Wright using his influence, Ellison was soon invited to join the project. While keeping him from being unemployed, the project gave him the opportunity to associate with young writers as well as with experienced authors.

At a salary of $22 a week, Ellison worked as a researcher on two separate projects. The first, known as "The Negro in New York," was an in-depth study of economic, political, and social conditions for blacks in the city. Ellison was responsible for interviewing hundreds of New Yorkers about their daily lives. He prepared numerous short memos on such topics as "Negro Instructors in New York Institutions of Higher Education" and "Great Riots of New York: A Complete Account of the Four Days of Draft Riots in 1863."

The second project on which Ellison worked also required many hours of walking through apartment complexes and interviewing local residents. Known as the "Living Lore Unit," this group of 27 writers talked with black New Yorkers from all backgrounds in an attempt to capture the story of the city in the words of its residents. The project was designed to record the living folklore of America's most diverse city.

Both of these assignments provided Ellison with hours of endless fascination. His work enabled him to meet New Yorkers from all walks of life. He listened carefully to their speech and determined that

Ellison said of author Richard Wright, "To encounter the possessor of such literary talent and have him make me his friend and confidant—that was indeed an exciting and inspiring experience."

Diplomat Ralph Bunche (left) attends a United Nations conference. His influence helped many blacks—including Ellison—to land a job with the Federal Writers' Project in 1938.

"the character of a people is revealed in their speech." He later based many of the idioms, rhythms, and jokes that appear in his stories on things he heard during these interviews. Because blacks from all over the country had migrated to New York, the city offered the astute researcher access to many of America's different regions.

One day Ellison was making the rounds in an apartment building in San Juan Hill, a black district that was later bulldozed to make way for Lincoln Center, New York's cultural center. From the hallway he could hear a heated argument going on inside an apartment. He could hardly believe the topic of the swearing and yelling: in a run-down apartment build-ing, he was listening to four men argue about opera. They were debating which of two celebrated singers at the Metropolitan Opera was the superior soprano. Ellison later said, "The subject of their contention confounded all my assumptions regarding the corre-lation between educational levels, class, race, and the possession of conscious culture."

When Ellison entered the apartment, he found four men with soot-covered faces, dressed in faded blue overalls, with a coal scoop beside each man. These men hauled coal for a living, but they also worked as extras at the opera and had become devoted opera fans.

The meaning of Hazel Harrison's parable about playing one's best "even if it's only in the waiting room at Chehaw Station" became particularly clear to Ellison. An artist should never make any assump-tions about his audience. Every effort should be an artists's best, for someone who appears ignorant but is really quite knowledgeable might be attending. After talking to these four men in the San Juan Hill apart-ment, Ellison understood that a commitment to art meant devoting himself to his work 24 hours a day.

This newly found commitment began to center around short story writing, and in September 1939 "Slick Gonna Learn" became the first of Ellison's short stories to achieve publication. It is a brief tale about a black southern worker who loses his job and gets into trouble with the law. After being treated in various ways by whites, he ultimately learns that he should not generalize about people.

"Slick Gonna Learn" was followed in print by "The Birthmark" and "Afternoon," both published in 1940. Like many of Ellison's early stories, these two works focus on racial encounters. "The Birth-mark" is about a young southerner who has to face the fact that his brother has been lynched. "After-

noon" is the first of several stories by Ellison to feature Buster and Riley, two adventurous boys growing up in Oklahoma.

Ellison often began to work on a story by writing down the themes that he wanted the story to include. He then developed plots and characters around these themes. He felt that by writing short stories in this manner, he was preparing himself for his ultimate goal as a writer: to produce a novel. According to

Ellison, a novel "demands that the writer be willing to look at both sides of character and issues—at least while he's working. You might say that the form of the novel imposes its morality upon the novelist by demanding a complexity of vision and an openness to the variety of depth of experience."

As Ellison developed as a writer, a novel would someday serve as the perfect medium for him to express his ideas. ❧

6

ART
AND ACTION

❧

ELLISON CONTINUED to write stories and work for the Works Progress Administration until 1942, when he left to serve as the managing editor for a new periodical called the *Negro Quarterly*. The magazine, which he worked on for almost a year before it folded, had been founded by writers who were attempting to break away from Harlem's strong Communist community. Although many of Ellison's close friends, including Richard Wright, were members of the Communist party, Ellison never joined. He had studied Communist writings and doctrine during his first years in New York, and had attended various social functions and conventions to support leftist causes, including a trip in the spring of 1940 to Washington, D.C., to attend the Third National Negro Congress. His visit to this congress inspired an article entitled "A Congress Jim Crow Didn't Attend" for *New Masses*. Championing the new black leadership that he had witnessed at the congress, he wrote: "Suddenly I realized that the age of the Negro hero had returned to American life."

During this politically active period in Ellison's life, he also wrote articles and book reviews for such radical periodicals as *New Challenge*, *Direction*, and *Negro Quarterly*. Always socially conscious, he was

An antiwar demonstration in Harlem calls for blacks and whites to unite in the fight against fascism.

President Franklin Roosevelt's administration established a Jim Crow army to fight in World War II. Ellison was angered by this segregation of blacks and whites.

supplied with a great deal of material to focus on as a writer thanks to the depression. He saw "the grinding impact of the depression upon the aroused Negro people was transforming its folk consciousness into a working class awareness," and he felt a responsibility to speak for these oppressed blacks.

"The stimulus that existed in New York during the thirties was by no means limited to art; it was also connected with politics," Ellison maintained. But by the early 1940s he had decided to reduce his ties with the Communist party and had begun to seek a more independent political outlook. As a writer, he was uncomfortable with the set programs championed by Communist writers like Richard Wright. He preferred to focus on a fictional world in which hope and possibilities existed. He said:

> Literature teaches us that mankind has always defined itself *against* the negatives thrown it by both society and the universe. It is the human will, human hope, and human effort which make the difference. Let's not forget that the great tragedies not only treat of negative matters, of violence, brutalities, defeats, but they treat them within a context of man's will to act, to challenge reality and to snatch triumph from the teeth of destruction.

Ellison's break with Communist ideology coincided with the start of World War II. President Franklin Delano Roosevelt's administration had established a Jim Crow army that separated white and black soldiers into different units, and many blacks—outraged at this blatant segregation—reacted against an administration they had grown to trust during the depression. Ellison was among those who were dismayed by the government's decision to separate white and black soldiers. But America's Communist party leaders endorsed the Jim Crow army, leaving Ellison bitterly disappointed in the party.

The depression marked a time of increased social awareness as a large number of people fell victim to oppression and poverty.

In 1943 Ellison decided to join the merchant marine because, he said, he "wanted to contribute to the war, but didn't want to be in a Jim Crow army." The merchant marine is a fleet of vessels engaged in business rather than military operations. During World War II, the merchant marine of the United States helped to transport men and material across the Atlantic and the Pacific.

In the racially mixed merchant marine, Ellison worked as a cook and a baker aboard a ship for almost two years. His first trip to Europe with the merchant marine was especially difficult. His convoy was attacked by the Nazis. Bad weather made the journey even more dangerous. But like his father, who had fought both in the Caribbean and in Asia during the 1890s and early 1900s, Ellison was proud to serve his country.

Life in the merchant marine consisted of long tours of duty at sea and relatively long leaves which Ellison spent in New York. On one of his leaves in

Black soldiers such as the ones shown here resented the formation of segregated armies during World War II.

1944, he met Fanny McConnell. A mutual friend had suggested to both Ellison and McConnell that they might enjoy each other's company. After first talking on the phone, they decided to meet at Frank's Restaurant on 125th Street in Harlem. Because they had never seen each other, he told her what color coat he was going to wear and she told him what the color of her dress would be. They met in front of the restaurant and immediately felt comfortable with one another.

McConnell assumed that the 30-year-old Ellison had hardly any money because he was a writer, so she ordered the cheapest item on the menu, even though she knew it wasn't one of Frank's specialties. So as not to embarrass her, Ellison ordered the same thing. But they soon forgot about their food as they became engrossed in a conversation about writing.

Ellison first met his future wife, Fanny McConnell, at Frank's Restaurant in Harlem in 1944. They were married two years later.

Secretary of the National Association for the Advancement of Colored People, James Weldon Johnson was also a well-respected songwriter and author. Ellison's wife, Fanny, worked for him while she was in college.

After their first meeting, Ellison began to call on Fanny McConnell regularly. They were eventually married in 1946. (Ellison was briefly married in the late 1930s. His first marriage ended in divorce.)

In many ways Ellison and Fanny McConnell were perfect for each other. Like her husband, Fanny had spent much of her childhood reading books and magazines and dreaming of a better life in a faraway place. She had been raised in Colorado and in Chicago, Illinois, and had attended Fisk University in Nashville, Tennessee. In college she had worked as a secretary for James Weldon Johnson, a well-respected author and diplomat who was a leading force during the early days of the National Association for the Advancement of Colored People (NAACP). Fanny had thought at one time of becoming a writer, but she decided not to pursue this ambition because she feared that she lacked the ability.

While Ellison was at sea, he found the time to write short stories and book reviews. Among the stories that he wrote during this period was "King of the Bingo Game." One of his most powerful tales, "King of the Bingo Game" is about an out-of-work young man who is struggling to right himself. He gains a sense of identity only after he refuses to take part in a role that others want him to play.

Other stories that Ellison wrote around this time— including "Mister Toussan," "That I Had the Wings," and "In a Strange Country"—helped him in 1944 to win a Rosenwald Fellowship to write a novel. With the money he earned in the merchant marine and the $1,500 from the fellowship, he became financially solvent for the first time in many years.

The Rosenwald Fellowship enabled Ellison to work on a wartime novel chronicling the adventures and hardships of a black Air Force pilot shot down over Nazi Germany. Captured by the Nazis, the pilot is taken to a prisoner-of-war camp, where he is confined

Members of the 99th U.S. Fighter Squadron, the first all-black outfit in the Air Force. Ellison finished but never published his novel about a black pilot in World War II.

with other American soldiers. Because he is the highest-ranking officer in the camp, he becomes the group's leader and spokesman. Many of the white prisoners of war resent his position of authority, and a Nazi camp official tries to exploit the already tense situation between the black officer and white soldiers by pitting them against each other. Accordingly, the black officer is faced with two problems. He not only has to deal with the Nazis, but he must lead a group of unfriendly Americans through their time in the prisoner-of-war camp.

Ellison developed the idea for the book after talking to some of his Tuskegee friends who became combat pilots. In writing this story, he hoped to make a statement about the Jim Crow army, which expected black soldiers to risk their lives for a country that did not offer them the same rights as white soldiers. The story seemed to be perfectly suited for a novel. According to Ellison, "The novel is a form which attempts to deal with the contradictions of life and ambivalence and ambiguities of value."

Although Ellison finished the novel, he was never completely satisfied with it. Only one section of the novel has ever been published, a section that Ellison turned into a short story titled "Flying Home." This story was published in 1944.

In the summer of 1945, Ellison returned to New York after a long tour of duty in the merchant marine. Exhausted and suffering from very low blood pressure, he decided to visit a friend's farm in Waitsfield, Vermont. Work on his war novel had come to a standstill, and his confidence in his abilities as a writer was at a low point.

As the weeks passed in Vermont, he regained his strength and confidence, and he was soon ready to begin work on the book that would launch his literary career. ❧

7

"I AM AN
INVISIBLE MAN"

─────── ✿ ───────

AT THE AGE of 31, Ellison spent part of his time in Vermont reading Lord Raglan's book *The Hero*, a study of historical and mythical heroes. In this book, Raglan theorizes about what makes a human being become a hero. He also examines the role that myths play in a hero's life.

After reading the book, Ellison began to think about leadership within America's black community. He asked himself why black society had been unable to produce effective leaders. He knew that he had to look at American society as a whole to discover why black society had been able to create so few heroes of its own.

One afternoon Ellison was sitting in an old barn, looking at Vermont's Green Mountains, and scribbling on a piece of paper. He then wrote five words that would change his life forever: "I am an invisible man." He was unsure of what these words meant, so he decided to see if he could explain what kind of character would call himself an invisible man. These five words and the explanation of the character that followed eventually became the beginning of Ellison's breakthrough novel, *Invisible Man*. He said, "I began to put other things with it. And pretty soon I had a novel going, and I began to work out of a conceptual outline on it. And as fast as I could work out the concepts, the incidents started flowing in on me."

Invisible Man has not gone out of print since it was first published in 1952.

INVISIBLE MAN: A SYNOPSIS

BEFORE ELLISON BEGAN *Invisible Man*, he had already written several short stories about young black men attempting to define themselves. Like these earlier stories, *Invisible Man* is about a young man's struggle to understand himself and the world around him. Yet there is more to the book than this one theme. It is a story of innocence, power, and corruption, and its many themes are so thoroughly developed that the young hero comes to represent all people who struggle to maintain their individuality.

Invisible Man is the story of an unnamed young black man who dreams of becoming a great spokesman for black people. He serves as the narrator of the novel. From an underground room, which is illuminated by exactly 1,369 lights, he tells us about the series of events that has caused him to become "invisible." He says:

> No, I am not a spook like those who haunted Edgar Allen Poe; nor am I one of your Hollywood-movie ectoplasms. I am a man of substance, of flesh and bone, fiber and liquids—and I might even be said to possess a mind. I am invisible, understand, simply because people refuse to see me.

Early in life, the narrator is told by his grandfather:

Son, after I'm gone I want you to keep up the good
fight. I never told you, but our life is a war and I have
been a traitor all my born days, a spy in the enemy's
country ever since I give up my gun back in the Re-
construction. Live with your head in the lion's mouth.
I want you to overcome 'em with yesses, undermine
'em with grins, agree 'em to death and destruction.

It is the narrator's practice of being agreeable that
eventually leads to his invisibility. For whenever he
acts agreeably, he winds up being victimized.

The first instance of the narrator being victimized
takes place while he is in high school. Having already
been selected to receive a scholarship to a black college, he is invited to deliver a speech before the local
white businessmen who are paying for the scholarship. Before making the speech, however, he is forced
to participate in a barbaric ritual known as the "battle
royal." Ten young blacks are put in a boxing ring,
blindfolded, and then told to fight each other until
only one of them is standing. The narrator says:

I was fighting automatically when suddenly I noticed
that one after another of the boys was leaving the ring.
I was surprised, filled with panic, as though I had been
left alone with an unknown danger. Then I understood.
The boys had arranged it among themselves. It was the
custom for the two boys left in the ring to slug it out
for the winner's prize. I discovered this too late. When
the bell sounded two men in tuxedos leaped into the
ring and removed the blindfold. I found myself facing
Tatlock, the biggest of the gang.

The narrator is knocked unconscious for a moment. Then, bleeding and barely able to stand, he
gives his speech, which is pointedly about blacks co-
operating with whites.

The narrator goes to an idyllic southern college dedicated to uplifting the black race with the help of rich white backers. In many ways, this college resembles Ellison's own school, Tuskegee. In fact, many of the novel's scenes and characters were loosely based on Ellison's own experiences in Oklahoma City, at Tuskegee, and in New York.

While at college, the narrator becomes the tour guide for Mr. Norton, an important white patron who is visiting the school. When Norton asks to see some of the countryside surrounding the school, the narrator knows that he is supposed to keep Norton near the school grounds, but he gives in to his guest's wish to see some new sights.

The narrator reluctantly introduces Norton to several blacks who do not aspire to the uplifting goal to which the school is dedicated. Norton first meets Jim Trueblood, a sharecropper who fathered his own daughter's child. Trueblood tells Norton that ever since his daughter bore the child, the blacks at the college have felt embarrassed by him and have tried to get him to move away from the area. He also tells Norton how local whites have encouraged him to stay on his farm. The implication is that the local white residents are jealous and fearful of the black college, and believe they can antagonize the blacks at the college by supporting the Trueblood family.

After several more incidents—including a visit to a saloon, where a brawl soon begins—the narrator brings Norton back to the school. The college's president, Dr. Bledsoe, finds out about Norton's unauthorized trip. The narrator says of his subsequent meeting with Bledsoe:

He looked at me as though I had committed the worst crime imaginable. "Don't you know we can't tolerate such a thing? I gave you an opportunity to serve one of our best white friends, a man who could make your fortune. But in return you dragged the entire race into the slime!"

Suddenly he reached for something beneath a pile of papers, an old leg shackle from slavery which he proudly called a "symbol of our progress."

"You've got to be disciplined, boy," he said. "There's no ifs and ands about it."

Bledsoe expels the narrator from school, although he is led to think that he has only been suspended. He plans to go to New York to work during the time of his supposed suspension, but before leaving, he picks up seven letters of recommendation written by Bledsoe and addressed to influential whites in New York. Because the letters are sealed, the student does not know that they tell their recipients not to hire their bearer.

Once in New York, the narrator is unable to find the kind of office position he wants. One of his letters is addressed to Mr. Emerson, whose son offers the narrator a job as a laborer in a paint factory. The narrator grudgingly takes the job , but during his first day at work he is injured and ends up in a hospital for several weeks. He eventually returns to Harlem, homeless and sick. He is taken in by a kindly woman named Mary and begins once again to believe that his future will turn out well.

Several months later, the narrator is out for a walk in Harlem when he sees an all-too-familiar sight: a crowd gathered to watch the eviction of an elderly couple from their apartment. The narrator begins to deliver an impromptu speech on the injustices that allow old people to be put out on the streets in the middle of winter. The crowd begins to riot. The narrator tries to escape, but not before he is noticed by a member of the Brotherhood, a liberal organization that bears some likeness to the Communist party.

The Brotherhood offers the narrator the position of chief organizer in Harlem, and he accepts. For the first time since his days in college, he feels that he can achieve greatness.

> The Brotherhood was a world within a world and I was determined to discover all its secrets and to advance as far as I could. I saw no limits, it was the one organization in the whole country in which I could reach the very top and I meant to get there. Even if it meant climbing a mountain of words. For now I had begun to believe, despite all the talk of science around me, that there was a magic in spoken words.

As a member of the Brotherhood, he is responsible for channeling the anger of Harlem's residents into nonviolent protests. He organizes rallies and delivers speeches about racial inequality and the fight for civil rights.

However, the narrator's ambition of becoming a great black leader is thwarted by the people he believes are helping him. He realizes that the mostly white Brotherhood is simply using him for their own ends. They do not care about him or the problems of blacks. He says, "Perhaps that's my greatest social crime, I've overstayed my hibernation, since there's a possibility that even an invisible man has a socially responsible role to play."

At the close of the book, the narrator is caught in Harlem during a race riot led by Ras the Destroyer, a violently anti-white rabble rouser. As a proponent of violence, Ras has been the narrator's chief rival in the campaign to unite Harlem's residents for political action. Ras insists:

> "Come in with us, mahn. We build a glorious movement of black people. *Black people!* What do they do, give you money? Who wahnt the damn stuff? Their money bleed black money, mahn. It's unclean! . . ."
>
> Clifton lunged toward him. I held him, shaking my head. "Come on, the man's crazy," I said, pulling on his arm.
>
> Ras struck his thighs with his fists. "Me crazy, mahn? Look at you two and look at me—is this sanity? Standing here in three shades of blackness! Three black men fighting in the street because of the white enslaver? Is that sanity? Is that consciousness, scientific understanding? Is that the modern black mahn of the twentieth century? Hell, mahn! Is it self-respect—black against black?"

The narrator is eventually forced to find shelter from Ras and his followers beneath the city's streets. He ultimately realizes:

> My problem was that I always tried to go in everyone's way but my own. I have also been called one thing and then another while no one really wished to hear what I called myself. So after years of trying to adopt the opinions of others I finally rebelled.

In refusing to accept the labels others have tried to pin on him, he becomes noticed by them. He begins to understand that the way for him to make himself visible is by establishing his own identity rather than letting others say what he should or should not be. ❧

8

IDENTITY CRISIS

*I*NVISIBLE MAN is a parable of the black man's plight in America, and the title of the book provides an interesting insight into that plight. During the 1930s and 1940s, white sociologists attributed the economic and social troubles of blacks to their "high visibility," saying that blacks are viewed by whites as being outside society because they have dark skin. These sociologists theorized that the economic and social woes faced by blacks were a direct result of their status as outsiders. Ellison found the term *high visibility* to be ironic. Although the black man is highly visible, he is treated by whites as if he does not exist, as if he were invisible rather than "highly" visible. Ellison writes in *Invisible Man*:

> You go along for years knowing something is wrong, then suddenly you discover that you're as transparent as air. At first you tell yourself that it's all a dirty joke, or that it's due to the "political situation." But deep down you come to suspect that you're yourself to blame, and you stand naked and shivering before the millions of eyes who look through you unseeingly.

Although the title *Invisible Man* refers to the second-class status of blacks in America, the narrator is

Harlem began to decline as a community after World War II. By 1950, many of its more notable residents had left the area.

also invisible to both blacks and whites because he refuses to define himself. Ellison said of *Invisible Man*:

> It's a novel about innocence and human error, a struggle through illusion to reality. Each section begins with a sheet of paper; each piece of paper is exchanged for another and contains a definition of his identity, or the social role he is to play as defined for him by others. But all say essentially the same thing, "keep this nigger boy running." Before he could have some voice in his own destiny he had to discard these old identities and illusions; his enlightenment couldn't come until then. Once he recognized the hole of darkness into which these papers put him, he has to burn them. That's the plan and intention.

The narrator lets others manipulate him, and they make him into the person they want him to be. Throughout the course of the novel, the narrator denies his true self. Thus, the narrator's invisibility not only suggests the invisibility and impotence of blacks in American society, but also the struggle of any individual to assert him- or herself.

Ellison has said of the novel's universal appeal:

> I conceived of the novel as an account, on the specific level, of a young Negro American's experience. But I hoped at the same time to write so well that anyone who shared everything except his racial identity could identify with it, because there was never any question in my mind that Negroes were human, and thus being human, their experience became metaphors for the experiences of other people.

Perhaps it is in this area that Ellison has contributed the most to American literature. All great literature allows readers from diverse backgrounds and different eras to identify with the main character. By casting a black character in a role that relates to both black and white readers, Ellison has shown that great characters in literature need not always be white. As the narrator of *Invisible Man* suggests, "Who knows but that, on the lower frequencies, I speak for you?"

This parade through Harlem in 1946 indicated a growing sense of pride in black values.

Ellison began *Invisible Man* in 1945, but it took him seven years before he finished working on it. Most of the writing was done after he returned from Vermont to New York and settled down in a Harlem apartment with his wife, Fanny, in 1946. Most of his fellowship money had already been spent, so he tried to find work as a free-lance photographer or by building high-fidelity sound systems. He also wrote book reviews. However, it was Fanny who was mainly responsible for supporting them during the first years of their marriage. She worked first as a secretary, and later became the executive director of the American Medical Center for Burma, an organization that raised funds to support the work of doctors in Burma.

Many of Ellison's neighbors questioned the integrity of a man who let his wife support him while he stayed home and wrote. Yet his wife continued to encourage him day, after day, knowing that someday his long hours at the writing table would pay off. Her faith in her husband proved to be well founded.

Some friends in New York also helped out Ellison with his writing. In 1946 Beatrice and Francis Steegmuller let him use their elegant Fifth Avenue office as a writer's studio while they went abroad. Ellison arrived at the office building with hundreds of other workers every day at 9:00 A.M. He rode the elevator to an eighth-floor office and spent the day writing. At lunch time, he was often the guest of Sam and Augusta Mann, two patrons of the arts. They encouraged Ellison in his writing and made sure that he was left undisturbed during the day. After a long day's work, he rode down the elevator with the other office workers at around 5:00 P.M. and made his way to the subway station to ride back to Harlem.

Ellison discovered that it was just as difficult to write in plush surroundings as it was in his cramped Harlem apartment. However, by sticking to a rigid schedule and keeping businessman's hours, he found that he was able to make great progress in the writing of his book.

The first chapter of *Invisible Man* was published in the British magazine *Horizon* in 1947. The following year, the first chapter also appeared in the American journal *Magazine of the Year*. The chapter received good reviews and encouraged Ellison to continue writing.

The entire text of *Invisible Man* was finally published in 1952. Ellison dedicated the book to his mother, who had seen to it that her son received a good education.

By the time of the book's completion, Ellison felt emotionally drained. He said of the book, "It was too difficult for me to get rid of, and not because I didn't write fast and wasn't inventive. But there was something else. There was a sense of isolation, a feeling that for all my concern to make it so, it couldn't possibly have much value to others. I thought that I would be lucky if I sold between five hundred and a thousand copies." Ellison's years of intense concentration on *Invisible Man* had left him blinded to the book's own merits. ❧

9

VISIBLE SUCCESS

❦

IN 1953 *Invisible Man* won the National Book Award, one of America's most prestigious literary prizes. Judged by a committee of writers and critics to be the best novel published in America in 1952, *Invisible Man* remained on the best-seller list for 13 weeks. This lengthy appearance was a tremendous accomplishment for a relatively unknown author who had written a work of noncommercial fiction. Critics and readers alike praised *Invisible Man* for its moving portrait of one man's struggle to understand himself.

The committee that selected *Invisible Man* for the 1953 National Book Award issued the following statement about the first novel by a black writer ever to be honored with the award:

> In it he shows us how invisible we all are to each other. With a positive exuberance of narrative gifts, he has broken away from the conventions and patterns of the tight "well-made" novel. Mr Ellison has the courage to take many literary risks, and he has succeeded with them.

The novel also won the Russwurm Award, given by the National Newspaper Publishers, and the Chicago Defender Award, honoring *Invisible Man* for "symbolizing the best in American Democracy."

A demonstration through the streets of Harlem offers a protest against the mistreatment of blacks in the South. Ellison said, "Today it is the black American who puts pressure upon the nation to live up to its ideals. It is he who gives creative tension to our struggle for justice."

Ellison (at left) receives the National Book Award in 1953. Also receiving an award were (from right to left) poet Archibald MacLeish and historian Bernard DeVoto.

Ellison's story explored issues never before discussed by a black writer. However, he has vigorously argued against interpreting it as simply a novel of racial protest. In creating a black hero with intellectual depth, he has transcended racial stereotypes. As his childhood belief in the Renaissance man would suggest, he was concerned with achieving a universal outlook on life, not a limited one.

After the initial excitement over the publication of *Invisible Man* died down, readers began to clamor for a second novel from Ellison. In 1955 he accepted a fellowship at the American Academy of Arts and Letters in Rome, where he and his wife spent the next two years. He taught in Rome and began to plan his second novel, maintaining, "I don't feel that I have exhausted the theme of invisibility." He started working in earnest on the book after he returned to New York in 1957. When he had trouble finishing it, he decided to satisfy his readers' thirst for more fiction by publishing parts of the novel as short stories. Known as the Hickman stories, these works—including "And Hickman Arrives," "The Roof, the Steeple and the People," "It Always Breaks Out," and "Juneteenth"—appeared in various magazines and journals.

Like *Invisible Man*, the Hickman stories explore such issues as race, identity, and spirituality. The two central characters are the Reverend Alonzo Zuber Hickman, an ex-jazz trombonist, and his adopted son,

Ellison went to Rome, Italy, in 1955 on a fellowship awarded by the American Academy of Arts and Letters.

The body of President John F. Kennedy is escorted up the steps of the Capitol Building to the Rotunda in Washington, D.C.

Bliss, a light-skinned boy who is often able to pass for white. Bliss is raised on the southern evangelical sermon circuit where his adopted father preaches. Hickman wants his adopted son to become a preacher, but Bliss eventually runs away. At some later time Bliss emerges in the North, where he becomes involved in politics.

As Ellison proceeded to work on his second novel through the late 1950s and early 1960s, he introduced a series of political assassinations into the plot. But the real-life assassinations of President John F. Kennedy in 1963, his brother, Senator Robert Kennedy, in 1968, and the Reverend Martin Luther King, Jr., in 1968 made Ellison feel as though his fiction was bearing too much of an eerie resemblance to real life. Although he attempted to rework the assassination

The funeral procession for slain civil-rights leader Martin Luther King, Jr., passes through the streets of Atlanta, Georgia.

The body of Senator Robert F. Kennedy is taken to Washington, D.C., for burial. His assassination closely followed the slaying of Martin Luther King, Jr.

scenes, the tragedy of these real slayings made it difficult for him to continue.

Instead of publishing a second novel as a follow-up to *Invisible Man*, Ellison published *Shadow and Act*, a collection of essays, in 1964. The book contained essays about literature, music, and American life. Since Ellison's days at the Federal Writers' Project, he had been interested in the study of American culture. In the pieces of nonfiction that appeared in *Shadow and Act*, he discussed the way in which aspects of black culture have been absorbed by white culture. Ellison argued against seeing black and white cultures as separate entities. Rather, he believed there has been an exchange of influences, ideas, and styles between the two cultures. He said, "I recognize no American culture which is not the partial creation of black people. I recognize no American style in literature, in dance, in music, even in the assembly-line process, which does not bear the mark of the American Negro."

The essays in *Shadow and Act* did little to correct a growing impression among the more radical members of the black community that Ellison was an "Uncle Tom"—a black who is eager to cooperate with and win the approval of whites. The term comes from the name of the central character in Harriet Beecher Stowe's 1852 novel *Uncle Tom's Cabin.*

To blacks in the 1960s who were calling for violent resistance to white culture, Ellison's assertion that black culture has blended with various European cultures to produce a distinctly American heritage was not very popular. They disagreed with Ellison's

Members of the Black Panthers, a militant organization advocating radical means to gain rights for blacks, give their "Black Power" salute.

criticism of anti-white sentiment, indicated by his portrayal of Ras the Destroyer in *Invisible Man*, and they objected to his apparent lack of interest in African culture.

But if Ellison's writing was unpopular with the more radical members of the black community, it was popular with almost everyone else. A poll taken by *Book Week* in 1965 of 200 of the nation's most respected writers, critics, and editors named *Invisible Man* as "the most distinguished work" to be written in the past 20 years.

During the 1960s, Ellison taught at Bard College in New York, Rutgers University in New Jersey, Yale University in Connecticut, the University of Chicago in Illinois, and the University of California at Berkeley. Sometimes he would encounter open hostility from black students who attended his lectures. Al-

An overwhelming majority of the black voters in the 1964 presidential election cast their ballot for Democratic candidate Lyndon Johnson.

President Lyndon Johnson (pictured on the sign) was criticized by many—including this group of demonstrators in the nation's capital—for expanding America's role in the Vietnam War.

though these students knew little about his personal views, they denounced him for some of his more controversial political stands. He was criticized for his support of President Lyndon Johnson, who inaugurated several important civil rights programs but also increased the scale of the Vietnam War. Ellison called Johnson "the greatest American President for the poor and for the Negroes," but this praise provoked blacks who wanted Ellison to renounce his support for Johnson in favor of some of the more radical black movements.

Ellison maintained that his role was one of an artist, not a political activist, even though he believed that artists have the power to effect social change. He has said that a novel can be "a raft of hope . . . that might help keep us afloat as we tried to negotiate the snags and whirlpools that mark our

A demonstrator taunts the military police during a 1967 anti-Vietnam War rally in Washington, D.C.

nation's vacillating course toward and away from the democratic ideal." Novels can suggest the possibility of change and improvement. They can offer readers a vision of the future minus the evils that mar the present, thereby encouraging readers to plan for a better future.

Realizing that a novel has the power to effect social change, Ellison has always viewed writing as a serious and important task, and has never taken his responsibilities as a writer lightly. He has pursued his craft with care and dedication. It is this insistence on being so diligent that made a turn of events in 1967 particularly upsetting to him.

According to Ellison, "Materially, psychologically, and culturally, part of the nation's heritage is Negro American, and whatever it becomes will be shaped in part by the Negro's presence."

Ellison is presented the Howells Medal for Fiction by fellow author John Cheever.

Early in the year Ellison and his wife bought a farm in Plainfield, Massachusetts, fulfilling a longtime dream of owning land in the country. Their farm, which featured a 200-year-old farmhouse, was a place where they planned on spending the summer to escape the hot and humid weather of New York City. Over a period of several months they repaired and decorated the house.

Then, in November 1967, tragedy struck. Their farmhouse burned to the ground. All they could do was stand by helplessly and watch. Lost were hundreds of personal possessions and momentos they had been collecting for more than 20 years. Although they rebuilt the house and were able to replace many of their possessions, there was one item lost in the fire that they could not replace. A year's worth of work on Ellison's second novel—about 350 manuscript pages—was gone forever. As of today, his second novel remains unfinished.

However, Ellison has been busy with other projects over the years. In 1970 he was awarded one of the most distinguished professorships in the nation when he was named the Albert Schweitzer Professor in the Humanities at New York University. He lectured at NYU twice a week on American literature for 10 years, becoming one of the university's most popular professors.

In 1970 Ellison was also presented with one of France's highest awards for an artist, the Chevalier de l'Ordre des Artes et Lettres. The ceremony was especially moving for him because the award was presented to him by André Malraux, who had become France's Minister of Cultural Affairs. It was on the steps of the Harlem YMCA in 1936 that Langston Hughes had given Ellison two Malraux novels, marking the beginning of Ellison's career in New York as a man of letters. ❦

10

RENAISSANCE MAN

❦

IN JUNE 1975, Ralph Ellison took an important trip back to Oklahoma City. His hometown had decided to name a new branch of the public library after him. The Ralph Ellison Branch Library now stands in what used to be an undeveloped area of fields and woods on the northeastern outskirts of the city. When Ellison was a boy, he used to hunt for rabbits in those fields. The library holds some 50,000 books and has seats for about 100 readers.

At the opening ceremonies, the mayor, state and local politicians, old friends, musicians, preachers, and children all turned out to witness the dedication of the new library. Ellison's wife, Fanny, and his brother, Herbert, who had settled in Los Angeles, were also there to help celebrate. One of the highlights of the day was the unveiling of a large sculpture of Ellison. The artist, Ed Wilson, a longtime friend of Ellison's, was present at the unveiling. The sculpture consists of two bronze images of Ellison. Wilson has said that the images show "Ellison the man of the world" and "Ellison the private man and contemplative artist."

Several speeches were made during the opening ceremonies. Hannah Atkins, a state representative, introduced Ellison to the crowd with this summation of his importance as a writer:

Ellison poses with Harvard University president Derek Bok in 1974, prior to receiving an honorary degree from the university.

In his essay, "Going to the Territory," Ellison wrote, "I realize how fortunate I am to have held on to literature as a medium for transcending the divisions of our society."

In all of Ralph Ellison's writings, we know that he is speaking to us about human beings, reflecting his deep understanding of man's inhumanity to man. He has delineated symbolically and directly the inequities and brutalities of our society. But in the midst of all this he has not become bitter. In the constant struggle for human liberation, he has provided us with sound philosophical reflections. Ralph Waldo Ellison, you have brought honor to Oklahoma, you have done us proud.

Ellison also made a speech in which he talked about his roots and the strange course of events that have led to his worldwide fame. He paid tribute to the effect that reading has had on his life and talked about his hopes that other youngsters would be stirred to dream of better lives within the walls of the Ralph Ellison Branch Library. He said:

I have no doubt that within these walls other writers—black, white, Indian—will emerge. . . . The library is a place where we are able to free ourselves from the limitations of today by becoming acquainted with what went on in the past—and thus project ourselves into the future.

Plans for the Ralph Ellison Branch Library in Oklahoma City, Oklahoma.

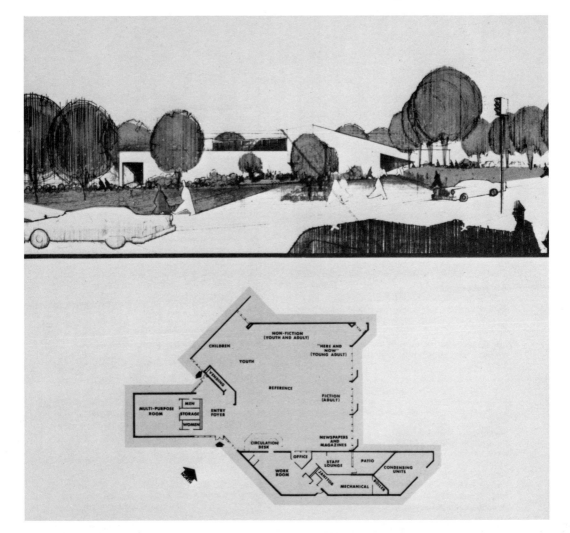

Ellison is honored at a political dinner in New York, along with Senator Walter Mondale (right) and secretary-treasurer of the AFL-CIO Lane Kirkland.

For Ellison, reading can be a step toward making one's dreams come true.

In addition to being a writer and teacher, Ellison has emerged as a leading cultural spokesman in America. Having served on numerous powerful commissions and committees, he has spoken in favor of cultural achievement and artistic freedom. He has often been the only black member to serve in these cultural groups, but he has said that his presence in these groups reminds America's decision makers that black people exist and that they too have needs. He has been an honorary consultant to the Library of Congress, a member of the Carnegie Commission on Educational Television, a charter member of the National Academy of Arts and Sciences, and a member of the National Institute of Arts of Letters. He has also served on the board of trustees of the Colonial Williamsburg Foundation, the John F. Kennedy Center for the Performing Arts, Bennington College, the Museum of the City of New York, and the New School for Social Research.

Ellison has received two of the nation's highest artistic awards for his contributions as a writer and thinker. In 1969 President Johnson awarded Ellison with the Medal of Freedom, and in 1985 President Ronald Reagan presented Ellison with the National Medal of Arts.

In 1986 *Going to the Territory*, Ellison's second collection of essays, was published. The title comes from "Goin' to the Nation, Going to the Terr'tor," a song about heading for the Oklahoma Territory, which was made popular by blues singer Bessie Smith. Many of the essays in this collection demonstrate his lifelong interest in the visual arts and music. There are essays on bandleader Duke Ellington and artist Romare Bearden as well as a piece on Ellison's early literary mentor, Richard Wright. Several essays discuss American literature and the function of the contemporary novel. But perhaps the most intriguing essays are those in which Ellison discusses his Oklahoma roots. They reveal his affection for his home state, where his interest in the arts first took hold.

Ellison's accomplishments since his days as a boy growing up in Oklahoma are a testament to his inner strength and discipline. Dedicating himself to the pursuit of his ideals, he has refused to waver from his boyhood goal of becoming a well-rounded person. From his earliest days in New York, when he had no place to sleep and hardly enough money to get by, to his current position as a leading figure in America's literary scene, he has shown the resolve to be conscientious and uncompromising. Truly self-made, Ralph Ellison has become not only a modern hero but a Renaissance man. ◉

CHRONOLOGY

March 1, 1914	Born Ralph Waldo Ellison in Oklahoma City, Oklahoma
1917	Father dies
1933	Ellison enters Tuskegee Institute in Alabama
June 5, 1936	Arrives in New York City
1937	Mother dies
1938	Ellison begins working for the Federal Writers' Project
1942	Becomes managing editor of *The Negro Quarterly*
1943	Joins the merchant marine
1944	Awarded a Rosenwald Fellowship to write a novel
1945	Begins working on *Invisible Man*
1946	Marries Fanny McConnell
1952	*Invisible Man* is published
1953	Ellison receives the National Book Award for *Invisible Man*
1955	Becomes a fellow at the American Academy of Arts and Letters in Rome
1964	*Shadow and Act* is published
1967	Fire at country home in Plainfield, Massachusetts, destroys part of his second novel
1969	Awarded the Medal of Freedom
1970	Awarded the Chevalier de l'Ordre des Artes et Lettres in France
	Becomes Albert Schweitzer Professor in the Humanities at New York University
1985	Awarded the National Medal of Arts
1986	*Going to the Territory* is published

FURTHER READING

Anderson, Jervis. "Going to the Territory." *The New Yorker* 52 (November 22, 1976): 55–108.

———. *This Was Harlem*. New York: Farrar, Straus, and Giroux, 1982.

Bloom, Harold, ed. *Ralph Ellison*. New York: Chelsea House Publishers, 1986.

Ellison, Ralph. *Going to the Territory*. New York: Random House, 1986.

———. *Invisible Man*. New York: Random House, 1952.

———. *Shadow and Act*. New York: Random House, 1964.

Hersey, John, ed. *Ralph Ellison: A Collection of Critical Essays*. Englewood Cliffs, NJ: Prentice-Hall, 1970.

O'Meally, Robert G. *The Craft of Ralph Ellison*. Cambridge, Mass.: Harvard University Press, 1980.

Reilly, John M., ed. *Twentieth Century Interpretations of Invisible Man: A Collection of Critical Essays*. Englewood Cliffs, NJ: Prentice-Hall, 1970.

INDEX

PICTURE CREDITS

JACK BISHOP is an associate editor at Chelsea House, working on the Chelsea House Library of Literary Criticism. A graduate of Yale with a degree in English, he has written for the *Village Voice*.

NATHAN IRVIN HUGGINS is W.E.B. Du Bois Professor of History and Director of the W.E.B. Du Bois Institute for Afro-American Research at Harvard University. He previously taught at Columbia University. Professor Huggins is the author of numerous books, including *Black Odyssey: The Afro-American Ordeal in Slavery, The Harlem Renaissance,* and *Slave and Citizen: The Life of Frederick Douglass.*